I DO, I DON'T, WE WILL,
WE WON'T

What is Marriage?

I DO, I DON'T, WE WILL,
WE WON'T
What is Marriage?

by
TYRONE THOMPSON
(A.K.A. PAPA SAN)

Noahs Ark Publishing Service
Beverly Hills, California

I Do, I Don't, We Will, We Won't: What is Marriage?

ISBN 978-1-7357447-6-6

Copyright © 2022 by Tyrone Thompson

Published by:
Noahs Ark Publishing Service
8549 Wilshire Blvd., Suite 1442
Beverly Hills, CA 90211

www.noahsarkpublishing.com

Creative Input: Laval Belle
Editor: Elyse Wietstock
Pre-Editing: Carolyn Billups
Graphic Design: Christopher C. White
Interior Design: Andrea Reider

This book is dedicated to my wife, Pastor Debbie Alana Brown-Thompson. Words are just not enough to describe how much I love, appreciate, honor, and respect this GOOD THING God has blessed me with.

TABLE OF CONTENTS

FOREWORD

It is not often we find a book on marriage that is sharing the things we need to know. "Papa San" takes this one deep into relationships and talks about challenges couples will be confronted with. Whether you have just gotten married or have been together for years, it will enrich your journey together. We truly recommend this book for guidance.

~ Billy Davis, Jr. & Marilyn McCoo

INTRODUCTION

I was deeply motivated to write *I Do I Don't, We Will We Won't* for several reasons. The subject matter cries out from my soul's personal experience! I have seen so many homes divided, children separated from their parents, and grown men and women struggling to find the glue that holds a marriage together. As a Kingdom Leader, I believe it is my responsibility to inform others regarding the beauty in marriage.

When it comes to the marriage relationship there are three parties involved and three steps in the ever-growing process. The three parties in a marriage include one man, one woman, and God. The three steps to marriage are: *Engagement*, which is a promise to marry the one you love. *Covenant*, a commitment you have made with each other and *Vow*, the commitment both parties make before God.

I Do I Don't, We Will We Won't educates by using my personal experiences, including the difficulties and hard times suffered in my own marriage. It also expresses how the love of God keeps us together and committed to each other. For several years my wife Debbie and I have received feedback, questions, and concerns from married couples regarding our marital teaching program, Weddi-Wednesday. Weddi-Wednesday elevates mindsets, encourages building strong foundational marriages, and tackles the most difficult questions. In 2019 we hosted our first Marriage

Cruise which included seminars and teachings aimed at rekindling the fire in marriages. The event was a powerful success. We achieved our goal by celebrating married couples and hosting a vow renewal which brought refreshment to their relationships.

As a Pastor, part of my assignment is to help couples remain committed to their covenant by pointing them to God, who can navigate their lives toward success. It is a good thing to interact with others and share my personal life experiences along with the lessons I've learned. Doing so led me to make necessary adjustments, which helped my wife and I achieve the marriage we desired. I believe this book will reveal painful yet necessary truths. Ultimately, with mutual cooperation, these realities can become strong foundation stones for healthy relationships to build upon.

CHAPTER ONE

BUILDING ON A LOVE FOUNDATION

Question. What is marriage?

Marriage is a covenant between God, one man, and one woman.

The institution of marriage is the creation of God. The marriage arrangement is built on three important principles. The first principle is a promise that solidifies the engagement. The second principle are vows that reflect the couple's commitment to go the distance through acts of obedience. The third important principle is the covenant that joins both man and woman together, with God being the center, to hold the marriage together for life.

Marriage is a lifetime commitment for both the man and woman involved. This is why it's very important to know whom we are going to share the rest of our life with, so the relationship doesn't short circuit. I wrote this book to tell you some things that can save your marriage from going down the drain.

Let's keep in mind that marriage was instituted by God to also help to establish His plans and purpose on the earth. This is why marriage is so important. God wired His perfect will through families. If you look through the scriptures, you will see how God wired His purpose through Abraham, Isaac, and Jacob/ Israel. These patriarchs are the roots from which the nation of Israel sprang. Marriage must be established on a solid foundation. Some may ask, "What is that foundation?" But I would rather you ask, "*Who* is this foundation?" This foundation is Jesus Christ, who is love!

God's love is called *agape,* which is an unconditional love. We can't earn agape love, but we need to demonstrate it in marriage as it flows from the Greater One (God) who lives inside of every born-again believer. It should be given unconditionally to one another in a marriage, not only when good deeds are done, but at all times. I wish all married couples had gotten that before they said, "I DO." This would have prevented many from saying, "I DON'T." Before you say, "I WILL," please seek wise counsel to prevent you from saying, "I WON'T."

Often people today get married under a false kind of love that comes with conditions. Many believe that a worldly type of love is driven by conditions. Those conditions place the married couple under contract instead of covenant. Those types of love only survive by feeding itself with personal desires, not the true unconditional love that is needed for marriage, which is *agape.*

No wonder some married couples who said they were in love are divorcing on the grounds of irreconcilable differences, they are no longer in love. Where did the love go? How did we lose our love for each other? The truth is this worldly way of love was not true love in the first place. Sensual love is hard to sustain in a lifetime marriage. I call it a "Hot Cup of Tea" love; it will cool before you know it. This love can start with great passion and drive, but eventually grows cold like ice and freezes even in its prime. If the man's money runs out, she leaves him. If the woman loses her shape after having his children, he leaves her for a younger girl. As a result, divorce rates skyrocket and families are divided, leaving children with only one parent in the home. Young girls seek out older men and young boys join gangs, searching for father figures. Many of those young men may find themselves in prison or losing their lives prematurely.

The writer Paul describes the type of love we should build on:

*"**4** Charity suffereth long, and is kind; charity envieth not; charity vaunteth not itself, is not puffed up, **5** Doth not behave itself unseemly, seeketh not her own, is not easily provoked, thinketh no evil; **6** Rejoiceth not in iniquity, but rejoiceth in the truth;**7** Beareth all things, believeth all things, hopeth all things, endureth all things".* (1 Corinthians 13:4-7)[1]

The scripture above displays the loving nature of our God. This love is empty of selfishness and avails itself to serve others without asking for a favor in return. This agape love is the foundation every marriage should build on in order to experience a successful marriage. When one party is weak, the agape love in the other will hold things together. It demonstrates a high level of spiritual maturity in Christ when God's love is displayed in marriage. For example, the qualification for a bishop in scripture is as follows:

*"**2** A bishop then must be blameless, the husband of one wife, vigilant, sober, of good behaviour, given to hospitality, apt to teach; **3** Not given to wine, no striker, not greedy of filthy lucre; but patient, not a brawler, not covetous; **4** One that ruleth well his own house, having his children in subjection with all gravity; **5** (For if a man know not how to rule his own house, how shall he take care of the church of God?)"* (1 Timothy 3:2-5)

---

[1] All referenced scriptures are taken from the King James Version.

What happens in a home reflects a healthy or unhealthy marriage. I believe a Christ-centered home reflects a healthy marriage. Our relationship with Christ should mirror our relationship with our family life at home.

"25 Husbands, love your wives, even as Christ also loved the church, and gave himself for it; 26 That he might sanctify and cleanse it with the washing of water by the word, 27 That he might present it to himself a glorious church, not having spot, or wrinkle, or any such thing; but that it should be holy and without blemish." (Ephesians 5:25-27)

How does Christ love His church? Remember, His love towards us is unconditional. The husband carries the same responsibility to love his wife as Christ loves us, His church. The wife also has a responsibility to be a helpmeet to her husband that makes it easy for him to carry out his responsibility in marriage under agape love.

"33 Nevertheless, let every one of you in particular so love his wife even as himself; and the wife see that she reverences her husband." (Ephesians 5:33)

Keep in mind, God provided us the best marriage counselor that we will ever need, the Holy Spirit. The Holy Spirit will assist us in every area of our lives to help us live the life Jesus designed for us to live.

"26 But the Comforter, which is the Holy Ghost, whom the Father will send in my name, he shall teach you all things, and bring all things to your remembrance, whatsoever I have said unto you." (John 14:26)

What the world calls love is not God's definition of true love. The world's love is conditional, which can leave us with no fuel in our relational tank. We must use the love in our hearts that God has given to us through the Holy Spirit and allow Him to help us live out what is already inside of us. Understanding the purpose of agape love in marriage will help us see God's love from His perspective. God is patient with us and long-suffering in the same way we must be toward each other in our marriages.

What is patience?

Patience is displaying the right attitude while waiting.

> *"4 But let patience have its perfect work, that you may be perfect and complete, lacking nothing."* (James 1:4)

What does it mean to be long-suffering?

Patiently enduring lasting offense or hardship. Long-suffering can also be defined as being persecuted by someone while waiting patiently for that person to turn to God.

Having these qualities will take you on an amazing journey that will turn out to be a great legacy for others to follow. Let agape love be the foundation on which you build your marriage.

Love causes you to **be faithful.**

> *"5 And hope does not put us to shame, because God's love has been poured out into our hearts through the Holy Spirit, who has been given to us."* (Romans 5:5)

If your foundation is unstable, I recommend demolishing the entire structure and rebuilding on Godly principles. If you are in a reconstruction period, be encouraged. There is still great hope for you. Our God is a God of restoration. Just know God can rekindle every fire and bring back to life anything that is dead or dormant in your marriage. Nothing is impossible with Christ Jesus!

CHAPTER TWO

UNINVITED GUESTS

There are some uninvited guests that don't belong in your marriage. If those guests are not addressed early, they will drive a wedge between you and your spouse. Marriage counseling is very important because it helps weed out some of these uninvited guests in your relationships.

Who are some of the uninvited guests on our guest lists?

Pride
Selfishness
High expectations of each other
Unforgiveness

The list goes on and on. Let me point out some of the main occupiers that can crush a marriage to powder.

Past Issues

If you are not careful, failed relationships from your past will dictate your present marriage and its future. Sometimes the woman is looking for a man to meet her needs, trying to fulfill what was lacking in her previous relationship. The same is true for the man. The problem is both are robbing each other of a fair start. With this mindset, it would be difficult for both parties to enter into a relationship and invest in each other wisely. Instead, you approach the relationship with unrealistic expectations of each other. The focus is what you can get out of the union before investing in it. Remember, marriage is a "give-give" relationship. She comes in giving and he comes in giving. You cannot be looking for handouts, but looking for ways to invest in your marriage, to match the dreams in your heart and mind.

Your Parents' Luggage

This is another uninvited guest we need to look at closely. These are habits that we bring from home, habits you have learned from your parents that have no biblical basis or structure. If not corrected, you can find yourselves living your parents' failures all over again. The result will be the same, but no one knows who to blame. Check to see if you are carrying your parents' unnecessary luggage with you. Our parents deserve respect and honor. You can take Godly advice from your parents, but keep in mind, your spouse is your lifelong partner who should not be overlooked.

> *"24 Therefore, shall a man leave his father and his mother, and shall cleave unto his wife: and they shall be one flesh"* (Genesis 2:24)

Independence

The day you both say, "I do," you are no longer a totally independent person. You share lifelong responsibilities. You can no longer eat what you want for yourself without being considerate of your lifetime partner. All selfishness must be locked out at the front door. Many married couples forget these things. Allowing that uninvited guest called *independence* only comes with one intention—to destroy your union of one. Independence does not mean you don't need another person. Ask yourself this question, "Why do you need a partner?" Marriage is not all about you, it's about us. We are in this together, looking out for each other. Trying to be independent in your marriage is not wise.

> *"11 Again, if two lie together, then they have heat: but how can one be warm alone?"* (Ecclesiastes 4:11)

Divorce

There is another guest that is more threatening than the others. This guest is the ringleader of all the others that work with it. It's the last one on the guest list. The previous guests set the stage for it. They create a negative atmosphere and cause great divisions, leaving the stench of hopelessness to give this last guest its grand entrance. It can be introduced as great hope, while dressed up in clothing of failure. The name of this guest is *divorce*. Let me tell you something about this uninvited guest.

Divorce comes in like a peacemaker. Divorce comes in as one who will remove the hurt and stop the pain. Divorce comes in to convince you that there is no other option. What divorce will not tell you is that it's costly and leaves more problems in a family than anything else. Especially with children who so desperately need their parents. Divorce splits the family wide open, removing the parents influence from their children. If you do start over, it will try to introduce itself again. It considers itself a champion in the systems of the world. Divorce leaves unattended wounds to infect the lives of others. It turns so many lives into an emotional drama. Departing from a past life, then creating a new fight, this cycle goes on into other relationships. Divorce costs money and births hatred and bitterness that costs so much more than the expectations of others. Divorce should not be a solution to run to, God must be first in all things.

One of the mistakes we make as married couples is that we leave things to fix themselves over time without confronting and dealing with them. Let me caution you on this—time does *not* heal all wounds. A wound left unattended over time will develop into gangrene. Anything infected with gangrene will be amputated. Go to God in prayer and ask Him for direction. He will give you the strength and ability to face the situation head on. Take the bold step to make things right. It is much better to fight the fire you have than to start a new one. Wounds left unattended breed unforgiveness, making your home a haunted house of bitterness. God did not design you to live in this manner. He wants you to live in peace, overflowing with His blessings.

Join your heart together with your spouse's in prayer and hold onto the promises of God. Your spouse is not the enemy. Remember, you are partners, you're on the same team. Recognizing these things makes the fight much easier. Why is this? Simple, you're now in agreement as one flesh; you're no longer divided. Who could be a better prayer partner than the person you are in covenant with?

"19 Again, I say unto you, that if two of you shall agree on earth as touching anything that they shall ask, it shall be done for them of my Father which is in heaven." (Matthew 18:19)

"14 And this is the confidence that we have in him, that, if we ask any thing according to his will, he heareth us." (1 John 5:14)

God's ears are open to our cries when it comes to His will in our lives. He will turn things around if you both are willing to submit yourselves to His Word. Go to Him with boldness and confidence because we are His children and He is our Father. When you receive Jesus Christ as your personal Lord and Savior by accepting His death, burial, and resurrection; having asked for forgiveness of your sins and believing in Him for your salvation—you become a part of His family. You will then have access to ABBA Himself. Take hold of the situation and pursue it with boldness.

My friends, again, please take note of these uninvited guests. Go to God in prayer together and ask Him to watch over the doors of your lives. Make sure these guests do not become a part of your family. There's no place for adoption, no place for uninvited guests.

CHAPTER THREE

MARRIAGE ON "E"

Marriage will take you on a lifelong journey and preparation is imperative. The support of counseling is a necessity. Without agape love and the proper building blocks, your marriage fuel will run low and impede you from going the distance. You will leave yourself open to the three Es that could lead to divorce in the long run.

The first E is *Emergency*. This is when the state of your marriage is in critical condition and desperately needs urgent help.

What can cause a state of emergency in marriage is a lack of service and overlooking the things that are most important to marriage. If a marriage reaches this critical condition, it needs immediate attention. A surgeon is needed, and surgery must be administered before the marriage flatlines. Even under those life-threatening circumstances, there is still hope because God's Word is the blueprint and prescription for a troubled marriage.

"1 I will lift up mine eyes unto the hills, from whence cometh my help. My help cometh from the Lord, which made heaven and earth" (Psalm 121:1)

God will reveal Himself mightily if you call on His name. He knows the places in your marriage that need to be restored.

Remember, He is the architect and the mechanic for our soul. When we refuse to deal with issues before they fester, we will suffer the consequences. We must surrender everything to God, and He will rebuild the bridges and broken walls of our lives. When your marriage is in the state of emergency you must stop, think, and seek direction. Seek the face of the Lord while you seek Godly counsel. You don't want to arrive at a place where your marriage is in a coma or becoming dysfunctional.

What does it mean when a marriage is in a coma?

You live in a house where there is no communication or movement toward resolution. You're just living without doing anything to resolve the issues. This is a marital coma. No one wants to make the first move to say, "I'm sorry," "I was wrong," or to seek help. Instead, one is waiting for the other to take the blame. You grant yourselves permission to ignore responsibilities by not addressing the situation. Even when you can see all the signs and signals, you turn a blind eye to them. Spiritual coma is when you and your spouse are hanging onto a sinking marriage. Just buying time while bracing yourselves for the worst. Waiting for someone to pull the plug, that's not the way God wants us to live. God did not institute marriage to function on life support.

The second **E** is *Empty*.

A healthy marriage is full of love when God is involved because He has what it takes to fuel our tanks for the distance. When a marriage is on "E" or empty, it is because the needs are being ignored.

No kiss, no hug, no smile, no laughter, and no intimacy. It's like you're living with a stranger. No affection, no fulfillment—just an empty marriage. You never want to get to that place. Don't ignore the signals. When you find yourself forgetting birthdays and anniversaries, when sex and kissing become just a mere fantasy, when the things you used to do together on a regular basis are now few and far between...you know the marriage is in trouble. Waiting for something bad to happen before you do anything good, that's not good. Waiting for a favor from your spouse before you treat them with love and respect are not good signs.

How can we avoid signs of denial?

Go back to where you started. Do the things you used to do that made you happy. Go out on dates and spend quality time with each other. Marriage is high maintenance because of its value.

The third **E** is *End*. My advice is don't give up!

When you're tired, frustrated, and confused, a new friend introduces itself: *End*, the third E. You think it cares about you and your children? It never thinks about the outcome and the backlash that will come when your home is divided. Let me ask you some questions, since you said you are tired of everything. Have you ever tried God? Have you ever consulted with Him? Did you seek His Word? Have you checked yourself? Think about these questions before making any drastic decision.

End gives you no other options. Your negative view of marriage can defeat you, your perception blinds you, and all you can see is the worst in the person you told "I do." Remember my friend, God is still in the business of repairing damaged goods. You should consult the surgeon. You should seek the Great Physician who is the architect of our souls.

Who is the surgeon?

Jesus is the Surgeon. He can put things back in line. He can replace what has been stolen. He will open your eyes to see clearly and heal the wounds in your heart. He will shine His light inside your marriage, get rid of the damages, and medicate you with His Word. Marriage was not designed to change you through hard times and circumstances. It was designed to keep us stable through those times. In other words, if everything is gone, we still have each other and God. When we have each other, we will bounce back and get stronger.

> *"9 Two are better than one; because they have a good reward for their labour. 10 For if they fall, the one will lift up his fellow: but woe to him that is alone when he falleth; for he hath not another to help him up. 11 Again, if two lie together, then they have heat: but how can one be warm alone? 12 And if one prevail against him, two shall withstand him; and a threefold cord is not quickly broken."* (Ecclesiastes 4:9-12)

What you feed each other can determine the outcome of your marriage.

What causes stress in the marriage is when one spouse allows their circumstances to change their feelings towards marriage. When the marriage is dying, it's time to change our diet plan.

How much time do you spend together? Past problems smell like stale food, and it's not good for you. This will send you to the emergency room.

What causes a marriage to be on life support?

Let me name a few things:

- **unresolved issues**
- **taking others for granted**
- **using the mistakes of the past against your spouse**

These can be very deadly in your marriage. They will create a breeding ground for tension, distrust, anger, and rage to build up inside of you which can one day lead to an explosion.

When a person does something wrong, the first move is to recognize the issue. Then take appropriate action to resolve it. Take responsibility, confess those sinful behaviors to God. Then admit those things to your spouse. This is where the healing process begins for the hurting person. This process helps release the built-up anger and deflates bitterness inside the one who is hurting.

Next, we must pay close attention to the way we misuse what rightfully belongs to your spouse. There is nothing anyone can do for your marriage to keep your marriage. In other words, if the wife thinks taking care of the household by cooking, cleaning, etc., is enough to keep the marriage, a helper can fulfill those chores as well. As for the husband who thinks opening the car door, etc., can keep the marriage, an assistant can do those things as well. None of those behaviors can keep a marriage together. What's really important is what your spouse provides in your marriage that no one else can. Some of these important things may be: affection, sex, or financial responsibilities.

A man can limit financial resources to his wife, which can put her in a place to provide for herself. This can take her away from true responsibilities, which can fuel resentment. She begins to feel like you are no longer needed. After all, she has now become an independent woman who can make her own decisions, creating her own little world that you are no longer a part of. This could lead to various problems that can eventually place the marriage on life support.

Now for the ladies, fasten your seat belts. I believe this will help you restore your marriage and make life much easier for you and your husband. Ladies, never use sex as an advantage over a man. This can be deadly and venomous for him. When a woman uses her body to gain advantage, it is like shooting yourself in the foot. This will put the man in a vulnerable position and an open target for the enemy.

> *3 Let the husband render to his wife the affection due her, and likewise also the wife to her husband. 4 The wife hath not power of her own body, but the husband: and likewise, also the husband hath not power of his own body, but the wife. 5 Defraud ye not one the other, except it be with consent for a time, that ye may give yourselves to fasting and prayer; and come together again, that Satan tempt you not for your incontinency"* (1 Corinthians 7:3-5)

God knows the dangers of a husband and wife not fulfilling their intimate duties towards each other. It can leave an open door for the enemy to invade. Temptation can present itself in an area of your life when there is a need. Believe it or not, they will not change anything. Sex is a need. Men need sex. Sex does a lot for the husband. Ladies, when you hold your husband in prison by withholding sex from him, you're forcing him to find other ways of satisfying his burning desires. Porn can become an escape route for some and adultery can introduce itself. If that husband is spiritually weak, this could lead to a nasty divorce. I am not making excuses, this is a fact. You can find the trails of evidence in a divorce court. The word of God is clear on adultery, which is a sin regardless of how it happens. No man should cheat on his wife. But wives, you are not out of the loop when you use your body as a weapon against your husband. These things can put your marriage on life support.

What does it mean when a marriage is on life support?

It is not surviving on its own. Something else is keeping it alive. When children are the only reason for a marriage to continue, it is an example of a marriage on life support. A marriage based on money is another example of a marriage on life support. A man can give his wife money but that does not mean it will resolve all issues. Even though money may be the root cause to some problems in your marriage, it will not bring resolution to all situations.

When your marriage is on life support you must recognize it needs immediate attention. Take responsibility for your actions and repent to God. Then apologize to your spouse and make every effort to earn their trust again.

Men! Kind words bring back your wife's smile. Value her opinions and share everything with her because you are one flesh before God. A woman always wants to feel safe. She is looking for that place of security from you. When you withhold your money, it speaks loudly to her and gives her a deaf ear to your voice. It makes her feel like there is a lack of trust and no self-worth. It's not about the money. It's about your heart and perception toward her.

Ladies! do not think a plate of food and house duties can solve your husband's issues. A man will eat your food, sleep in your clean bed, and still be upset with you. You must take the initiative to make things different. Do what it takes to satisfy his needs, open the door of intimacy, and let him feel a sense of belonging again. Be gentle, kind, and speak to him with respect. This will help to heal the wounds in his heart and mind. You can clearly see that both of you sometimes have different needs, but the healing process begins the same way.

*"**9** If we confess our sins, he is faithful and just to forgive us our sins, and to cleanse us from all unrighteousness"* (1 John 1:9)

*"**24** Pleasant words are as an honeycomb, sweet to the soul, and health to the bones"* (Proverbs 16:24)

CHAPTER FOUR

DANGER OF SURVIVAL MODE

S urvival mode is probably the most undetected issue we have in marriages. When you say, "I do" and step through the front door of your home for the first time with your spouse, survival mode can kick in immediately. Men, when your wife says she is pregnant with your first child, survival mode can kick in again. Why? Because as a father-to-be, you begin thinking about the future of your child and their wellbeing. You are no longer living for one, but for a family of two, three, or more for countless years. This kind of responsibility kicks you into high gear to work much harder. Your wife may even have to find a job as well to help out. Nothing is wrong with that, which makes it so tricky. We witness married couples working more than one job to take care of their children and home responsibilities.

It is a great thing to pay your bills to make sure the home front is safe. But think about it. How many hours do you have in a day, and how many of those hours do you use to work? Paying bills is very important but *paying attention* to each other is more profitable. Even though the car notes are paid up every month and kids' needs are taken care of through your hard work and dedication, the marriage oftentimes suffers. How did this happen after doing such a great job? Let me give you sound advice—**whatever you don't pay attention to will be cut off.** If the light and water bill is not paid up, both will be cut off. In the same way with your relationship, if you do not pay attention to each other, the marriage can be cut off as well.

When each party is overworked, it can rob every bit of intimacy from the marriage. You come home from your job while she is asleep, she got home from her job while you are asleep. This leaves the marriage without quality time while living from one moment to the next. We oftentimes see this lifestyle as a sacrifice, but every so often it kills marriages. When there is no intimacy in a marriage, loneliness kicks in. This can lead to all kinds of problems that will cost you greatly. You can get to a place of just tolerating each other, communicating only when necessary. The love in that marriage can grow cold before you recognize it, because it's already in **survival mode.**

Millions of marriages end in divorce because of survival mode. Today, so many people are trying to find out what caused their marriage to fail. Little did they know that survival mode blinded them from reality. Have you ever seen a couple who you thought had it all? The cars, the perfect house, great jobs, kids off to college and then they get a divorce? How could this happen? Surprisingly, there are no easy answers. Perhaps they simply grew apart. Many are surprised to hear this coming from those who they looked up to and admired. The truth is it is a common saying among divorced couple. They pay attention to other needs, and never pay attention to the needs of their own marriage. What they thought could keep things in place became the very thing that created a wedge in their relationship. Paying your personal bills are good, but keep in mind there are other needs to be met and it is to pay attention to each other.

It is much better to live an affordable lifestyle or downsize areas of your life. This lightens the weight on your shoulders allowing your marriage to breathe. Intimacy builds strong friendships and strengthens the relationship of the marriage. Spending time in prayer and in God's word, will strengthen your faith and a closer walk with Him. There is rest and peace in Jesus Christ, but we must trust Him and cast all our cares on Him.

"28 Come to Me, all you who labor and are heavy laden, and I will give you rest." (Matthew 11:28)

"7 Casting all your care upon him; for he careth for you." (1 Peter 5:7)

Spending time together creates more chemistry in the marriage. It will build a strong and binding relationship with your spouse. This will drive the bad residue out and allow love to take the wheel. Divorce will lose your address and uninvited guests will not invade your marriage. We have to trust God through the process. God's healing process make take some time, but rest assured He is always on time. He knows exactly what we need and where we are in our lives. He never makes mistakes or fails in any way; God is perfect.

"10 Declaring the end from the beginning, and from ancient times things that are not yet done, Saying, My counsel shall stand, And I will do all My pleasure" (Isaiah 46:10)

What I've learned in my life is this: money can make you backslide, not having money can make you backslide; but it all depends on your level of spiritual maturity in Christ. Whether having money or stone broke, we all need God. Couples who do not have money need God to get it. Those who are wealthy need Him to show them how to spend and keep it, and not allow it to become a god in their lives.

> *"24 No man can serve two masters: for either he will hate the one, and love the other; or else he will hold to the one, and despise the other. Ye cannot serve God and mammon"* (Matthew 6:24)

Survival mode is very hard to detect because you are doing so much of what is right. But in the end, your loss is so damaging; leaving you unfulfilled. You become strangers to each other, out of touch, numb to the pain of your spouse, making it hard to get along with the person you said, "I do" to. This can be avoided if we challenge ourselves to do what's right, by taking the initiative to make a change for the good.

How do we stay away from this trap? My answer is: Be satisfied with what you have. Celebrate what you achieved and give God thanks.

Check your priorities. God must be first, your spouse is second, and everything else will fall in its place. Purposely set time for each other weekly. You do not need a lot of money to go on a date night. Sharing one ice cream and walking the park can also help to strengthen your marriage. Things that you used to enjoy will certainly bring back some great memories. When there was no money, being with each other was so important to us. These activities will help fuel your marriage and keep the tank from falling to **E**. They will produce a life of balance and understanding and keep things moving in the right direction.

Look at what Christ says:

"15 And he said unto them, Take heed, and beware of covetousness: for a man's life consisteth not in the abundance of the things which he possesseth." (Luke 12:15)

This is a clear message to let you all know that life is not materialistic. We must place value on a higher priorities, strive to learn and enjoy the little you have. However, this carries less value than the abundance we have in God. You might be poor, but you will continue to advance in your relationship with your spouse, which is much better than being rich and divorced. For some, this might not fit their profile, but for those who belong to Christ, it should not be a problem.

Do not settle for a life that will haunt you in your older days. Love the one you have now. Don't give up the now for later. Many find themselves in a bed of loneliness, simply because of time not properly invested. You cannot get back lost moments; you cannot relive a life you did not live. You cannot regain what you did not attain. You cannot reverse what is in the past. Life is not made up of years, but of moments. Do not allow **survival mode** to kill your married life.

What are some necessary steps we should take to overcome survival mode?

Downsize to an affordable living because whatever is not a need becomes a strain. Do things you usually do to refuel the marriage. Take time to have clean fun and laughter. Place value on your marriage. Most importantly, pray and have daily devotion together regularly with the Lord.

CHAPTER FIVE

STAY IN YOUR LANE

As mentioned in Chapter One, a high level of spiritual maturity can be found in a marriage. A marriage is designed to express the love of God. Even through difficult times when it seems hopeless, God is still at work. This is how God sometimes stretches you like a bow. The further He stretches you, the further He can shoot you like an arrow. He's aiming for a target, and He never misses. In marriage, a husband and wife each have separate roles and functions in different lanes. Sometimes they see things through different lenses.

One of the most fundamental things everyone should know is that **only God knows all of you**. There is a portion of you that you don't know, but someone else does, because God revealed it to them. It could be your mother or your father, a close friend, or a pastor. It could be a wife or husband. There is a side of the husband that only the wife knows and vice versa. That is why listening to each other is essential in a marriage and could be an eye opener to hidden realities.

Counseling before marriage should be the first move after prayer. Seeking Godly counsel will prepare you with wisdom and understanding for the future ahead. Counseling can reveal another side of you that you were blinded to. This is why switching lanes and swapping roles creates so much confusion. If you allow the systems of this world to train or counsel you in your marriage without Godly counsel, you may find yourself disqualified on this marital journey. A Godly counselor can reveal who is an uninvited guest on your guest list. Don't give ear to every voice and opinion that carries no value, let the word of God have the final say.

In instances where something goes wrong and no one wants to admit their fault, then the blame game comes into play. Pointing fingers at each other becomes an easier way out, to avoid the onus of taking blame. This is another reason for Godly counseling.

"15 The way of a fool is right in his own eyes: but he that hearkeneth unto counsel is wise." (Proverbs 12:15)

We know many women these days are making more money than their male counterparts. I know for some men this can be intimidating, although it shouldn't be. There are men who do not know how to handle this truth so at times they approach it in error. For example, let's say your household monthly expenses are $13,000. Your wife makes $10,000 and you make $3,000 per month. This means, your wife is carrying most of the household expenses. How does a man handle this situation? A lot of men fail in this area because they pass their financial responsibilities to their wives which is unfair to her. When a man doesn't try to increase his income and expects his wife to continue shouldering the financial responsibilities this can be a problem in the marriage. Sometimes a man can feel inferior to their wife so they may not handle the situation with wisdom. In reality there are some men that do not understand their role as a husband. This leads to frustration that can drive a wedge in the marriage relationship.

It is very important to know your lane and what role you play in your marriage. We as men were created to lead, it is a part of our nature. Most women want a shoulder to lean on. When a woman feels she has to carry the weight of a home all the time, this could lead to frustration, fatigue, and stress. After a while she will start to vent her frustrations because she wants a man to lean on. A woman desires security, assurance, and affection. When these needs are not fulfilled for a woman in marriage, it can be harder for her to take care of the household.

How do you release that pressure?

Recognize that the financial responsibility in the home is mostly for the husband. Knowing this truth will give you a different approach to the situation. Instead of demanding things from her by reminding her of the monthly expenses, you should celebrate her by expressing your appreciation for her contribution on your behalf. In other words, let her know that the expenses are your responsibility, then assure her that you are doing the best you can to alleviate her from so much of the financial responsibilities. This approach will help remove emotional pressure. She will feel deeply appreciated when she does not see it as an obligation, but as a loving contribution from her heart. Now you're in your rightful position as a man who understands and fulfills his responsibilities.

My wife was my manager for many years, and I paid her a percentage of my earnings throughout those years. Whenever a bill was due, I never asked her to pay it. I took the initiative and paid our bills. I never let her feel she had an obligation to pay the bills of our household as they are my responsibilities. My wife also manages the household and sees to the welfare of our children as we play our roles to balance our marriage. She purchases things on her own that fill gaps I am not aware of at times. As my helpmeet, she watches over the affairs of our household which helps me to be the provider for our family. When a woman feels she has to carry most of the expenses, she can take on a leadership role unknowingly. A man can give her his position by passing on the responsibilities to her. If you find yourself in this position, go to your wife, let her know that you appreciate her for taking care of a great portion of your responsibilities, then relieve her from those obligations.

The bible depicts Christ as the head of the church and likewise, husbands have a responsibility to take care of their wives as her head. Marriage between a man and a woman should mirror the relationship between Christ and the church. This revelation will give a better understanding on how each person should play their role in the marriage. Understanding these tremendous truths of our roles and following the examples of our Lord Jesus Christ will shape and fashion us to represent Him well. A Christ-centered marriage reflects the relationship between Christ and His church.

Please do not exchange roles but seek to help each other in those roles when you see fit. Exercise appreciation to alleviate the pressure, live for Christ first then for each other. Everything will fall into the right place when your foundation is solid. "I DO" will not be exchanged for "I DON'T", "I WILL" will be not be exchanged for "I WON'T" and divorce will not have a voice but will be put to silence.

Husbands, do not give up your position because of a setback. Seek to do what it takes to fulfill your role with the guidance of the Holy Spirit. Set an example for your children and others to follow. Wives, do not take advantage of your husbands because you are more financially stable than him. This could crush his manhood, making it more difficult for him to be the leader. Lack of self-worth will kick in, failure and discouragement can take root that is so hard to get out of. Husbands, remember your wives need your shoulders to lean on. Do not let your pressure be a yoke around her neck. Be a pillow where she can rest her head, knowing that you got her back ready to take the hit for her. It's time to take the mask off and show the beauty that marriage truly possesses.

"25 Husbands, love your wives, even as Christ also loved the church, and gave himself for it; 26 That he might sanctify and cleanse it with the washing of water by the word, 27 That he might present it to himself a glorious church, not having spot, or wrinkle, or any such thing; but that it should be holy and without blemish." (Ephesians 5:25-27)

CHAPTER SIX

UNMASKING YOUR MARRIAGE

Marriage is a face-to-face and heart-to-heart relationship, but sometimes as married couples we don't see things eye to eye, we view things differently. One of the most fundamental things in a marriage relationship is to agree to disagree, giving respect to one another and valuing each other's opinion. We need each other to build a solid relationship. Marriage is a display, not a cover-up. If it is a cover-up, why get married in the first place? I am not saying that you should spill out your personal business to everyone, but I am saying when you say, "I do," you are no longer single or an independent person. To have a successful marriage we have to be real with God and with each other. Not having wise counsel defeats the purpose of a healthy marriage, creating a sick relationship that is bed ridden.

Marriage masking creates pretenders, believe it or not. It is a life of performance without purpose. Like it or not, the world is watching every move you make. This includes your friends, your family, and even your very children. The focus is to see how things will turn out. If that's the case, how long will your relationship continue if you're masking your marital problems? Creating your own fashion show, trying to distract everyone from seeing behind your marital curtain is not good. I agree that not everyone needs to see what's in your closet. Not every friend can keep a secret but keeping everyone at arm's length can lock out those whose wise counsel could help you as well. A life of masking turns you into a master entertainer. Everyone is dancing to your music, but they never bought your album. You perform to please everyone, but no one is singing your songs. Painting your world for everyone to see is only good for eyes and satisfying the walls it hangs on, while the marriage is stifling under the surface. Go to God in prayer concerning those issues, He will abundantly pardon.

> *"13 He that covereth his sins shall not prosper: but whoso confesseth and forsaketh them shall have mercy."* (Proverb 28:13)

Be real and walk in God's wisdom. Abandon the world's concept of marriage.

Sometimes we allow culture to get the best of us, refusing to let go of things we learned from childhood. We lie to cover up, then we blame others when we are exposed. These are learnt behaviors that cultures have introduced to us. We must undo them before they undo us. Has someone ever asked, "How are you?" and you gave them an answer that was not true? You might say, "All is fine," "We are doing great," "It's never been better," or "I'm living my dream!"

Do you know what kind of impression these responses leave on someone when your marriage is on suicide watch? Pretending everything is fine when it is not will hinder someone who desires to pray for you. Again, I am not saying that you should tell everyone about your private life but take the mask off and seek wise counsel. It's all about where the marriage is, every marriage does not have the same problems, the approach should be different based on the circumstances. Change your dialogue, be true and honest to the situation. If someone asks if all is well with you when you have been struggling, here are some answers you may consider:

"We have been through a lot, but now there's progress."

"I love the direction we're taking, and I am willing to learn more."

"We are taking it one day at a time; we will get there by the grace of God."

"I'm not where I want to be, but we are not where we were."

"It's good, but not perfect; we're striving to get there."

"We've had some great times... I am excited to see much more."

"God is in control; we will continue to follow Him."

"9 Lie not one to another, seeing that ye have put off the old man with his deeds;10 And have put on the new man, which is renewed in knowledge after the image of him that created him." (Colossians 3:9)

What kind of attitude are you displaying when you're around others?

Do you punch...then pamper?

Do you keep a distance...then touch?

Do you live in silence...then become a public speaker?

Do you live for pictures...and not purpose?

Do you live for profile...and not progress?

Do you live to please men? And not God?

Are you smiling while angry inside?

"25 Wherefore putting away lying, speak every man truth with his neighbour: for we are members one of another." (Ephesians 4:25)

Don't face-powder your life, it does not reflect the real you. Take the mask off and say to yourself, "Enough is enough." Unmasking yourself begins a new chapter in your life, it allows the light of Christ to shine in those dark areas. Living behind the mask puts cracks in the foundation of your marriage. Let honesty be your best policy. Be real from the get-go. Do not wait several years into the marriage before unmasking yourself. Do it NOW!

In other words, ladies, allow your spouse to see you naturally. Let him see what you truly look like. The very person you're hiding will be exposed when you wake up in the morning. Show him your natural beauty and be confident about it. Men, stop trying to impress your wives with lies about your status. If you have bad credit, say so. Let her see you for who you are. This will build trust that helps to hold everything together. Entering a new relationship should be for the right reasons. So, put your heart in the right place, be an open book. This way you can openly learn about each other. Keep your hearts pure toward each other.

What is a pure heart?

Before answering this question first let me ask another one. What does pure water look like? When water is pure, you can see everything in it. When water is dirty, you cannot see what is in it. It's the same way with your motives and your heart. Let your spouse see what is beyond the surface from the beginning.

Transparency creates real intimacy, but you have to take off your mask and allow your spouse to come in. Masking yourself is shutting the door and incarcerating the relationship for unprofitable reasons. When your spouse gets to know you inside out, there will be a deeper and greater appreciation for each other. This gives the relationship a fair chance for a lifetime together. Everyone deserves a fair chance. Do not provide room for each other's past failures. Let honesty and fairness be a part of your foundation. Keep things in the open with your spouse. Ask questions to get clarity on things you see or hear that you do not have answers for.

CHAPTER SEVEN

MARRIAGE, NOT AN AFTERTHOUGHT

aintaining your marriage is a lifetime practice of consistency, commitment, and responsibilities. An afterthought is a last resort. Treating your marriage as an afterthought is like having a side chick on layaway. If you wait until everything goes wrong before you pay attention to your marriage, divorce is at your doorstep with great anticipation. When a problem confronts you, face it with boldness. Tackle those areas head on together and keep in mind that you are a team player. So many of us think that longevity in a marriage can keep it going. That is not true, any marriage can fall apart if you leave it unattended. Kids, sex, and money do not guarantee a secure marriage.

The mistake that so many make is thinking that having children will keep the marriage together. Perhaps it's because they see the wedding ring as security. This idea plunges people into an afterthought lifestyle. It puts no value on the principles designed to keep a marriage, which are so important. Just because they said "I do," does not mean it's time to sit back hoping for the best. Marriage is a work-in-progress. The afterthought concept is crippling, placing your marriage in a wheelchair; it will have no strength to stand up under pressure. Every day you should take the initiative to see how you can improve your married life. Don't leave it on the side to survive on its own.

Here are some tips that I think will be helpful. My wife said this to me one day, and I quote, "You treat things the way you value them." When you place value on your marriage, you will see the equity in it. In other words, if you bought a house for $300,000 and in five years the value appraised to $700,000, would you sell it for the same $300,000? I can say without a doubt, "No!" You understand the value of the home you both invested in, how much more valuable is the marriage? All those years you both spent investing into each other; after sacrificing your time and strength by putting so much on the line, why do you want to call it quits? You play the blame game to divert from confrontation. It is so easy to point out a few bad things and ignore the multitude of good you both express to each other. Every home requires a paint job every now and then. Sometimes the roof leaks, along with other things that need to repair. I'm sure an expert in this field would advise you to do what it takes to maintain the value of your home.

Marriage is more valuable than divorce, but divorce can be more costly than marriage. The value of your spouse and the equity you both poured into each other is priceless. A divorce can cost you a lot of money, a lifetime of pain, grief, regret, and suffering which extends beyond both you and your spouse.

Ask yourself these questions before deciding to end your marriage.

- Did I pray about it?
- Is it worth it?
- Will this cost me more than I expect?

- What are the consequences?
- What does the word of God have to say about it?

"5 Trust in the Lord with all thine heart; and lean not unto thine own understanding. 6 In all thy ways acknowledge him, and he shall direct thy paths." (Proverbs 3:5-6)

Marriage was not an afterthought for God. He placed great value on marriage and used it to model what kind of relationship He has with His church. When marriage becomes an afterthought, it robs you of everything you both invested. Poor communication threatens the marriage, no chemistry, no spice, just living out the moments. So how do you get back on track? Both parties should seek God's direction, then take the necessary steps to make the relationship better. Here are a few suggestions that will provide Godly restoration.

Sweet words help keep the marriage together. You might try some expressions like:

For the husband, "Baby, I love you inside out." If that is true, why don't you say it? You should not allow someone else to say it for you. To the wife that means she's beautiful inside and out, pleasant and attractive, with an amazing personality.

For the wife, "Babe you are my lifelong dream that came true." If that's true, why won't you express it? To the husband this means she is not disappointed with him and has no intention of giving up on her dreams.

I love to tell my wife that she is under my arrest, and I love her without mercy.

Another quote is, "I wish I could turn back the clock and find you sooner to love you longer." This means you're intoxicated with God's love inside of you and you're willing to display it in the life of your spouse, never wanting to lose sight of it.

What about this one? "Giving up on you is giving up on me. I can't see me without you." This is a true definition of what one flesh means.

> *"28 So ought men to love their wives as their own bodies. He that loveth his wife loveth himself. 29 For no man ever yet hated his own flesh; but nourisheth and cherisheth it, even as the Lord the church."* (Ephesians 5:28-29)

Just want to remind you again that a successful marriage is built on the foundation of God's love.

Sometimes it is not so much the words, but the attitude. When a wife becomes a great fan and cheerleader who cheers her husband on, this is what you call a game changer. In other words, be the one who encourages him. Speak to him with respect. Men are built differently, it doesn't take much to satisfy us. It is no different from how we attire ourselves. Having a fresh haircut and sharp suit? We are done for the most part! Honor, respect, and encouragement are the main three things a man needs from a woman. However, women require more, in the same way they attire themselves…the dress that captured the eyes of her husband, grand hair style, nails manicured, makeup, well-groomed eyebrows, etc. In other words, wives need affection, security, and assurance, the same qualities the church finds in Christ, which are more important than the outward.

- Every business need money and integrity
- Trust is fed by honesty
- Friendship is built through loyalty

Every marriage needs all the above but only through Christ can we achieve these goals. When you treat your marriage like an afterthought it erases the spice, leaving no room for excitement. Nothing to explore, destroying all the ingredients that fuels the marriage. Living like roommates that have no interest in each other. To keep the spice in your marriage, exercise the elements of surprise. Don't always be predictable. There must be a side of you, that you both barely know in a good way. This is how you knock your mate off their feet. My wife arranged a renewal of vows for my 50th birthday. I was floored to see the style in which she put it together, doing the unexpected to keep the marriage exciting. Let your laughter play a major role, and don't take any moments for granted.

"22 A merry heart doeth good like a medicine: but a broken spirit drieth the bones." (Proverbs 17:22)

Don't be weird, rigid, stuck-up, or stiff-necked. Laughing releases stress. Please do not leave what is so precious as an afterthought. Take off the limits, do not handcuff your marriage with a handshake. How can you greet the one you love with a side hug when they are not a stranger? Putting your hand on the shoulder of your spouse or patting on the back, sometimes a fist bump is a sign of an afterthought lifestyle in a marriage. What about kissing and looking each other in the eyes? Create a spark and rekindle the fire again in your marriage. What about telling each other I love you every day? Planting those words like seeds will spring forth a harvest in your married life.

"18 Let thy fountain be blessed: and rejoice with the wife of thy youth.19 Let her be as the loving hind and pleasant roe; let her breasts satisfy thee at all times; and be thou ravished always with her love." (Proverbs 5:18-19)

God wants marriage to be enjoyable, capturing every moment and inspiring each other with agape love. Looking forward to each other with great anticipation, to do it all over again. An afterthought is an uninvited surprise to a boring marriage. In other words, if something bad happened in the relationship, do not allow it to fester before you address it. A problem that is not attended to could lead to a divorce or encourage cheating on each other. Let this be a wakeup call to give your marriage the attention it so desperately needs. Sometimes tears are a sign that something is long overdue. Things overlooked can invade your marriage in the future to come.

When you say, "I do," you both embark on an assignment. You become team players working to complement each other. Watch each other's back even if you don't see eye to eye. Don't live for holidays, live for every day. Every kiss is special, the times you share cannot be replaced. Learn to set the mood days before, to create an atmosphere of love and affection…let those moments tell their own story. Plant and create great memories that will live on with you as you grow old together. Take your marriage seriously, do not take it for granted.

CHAPTER EIGHT

ROLE PLAY

A successful marriage is understanding the meaning of "role play." Role play is allowing each person to be themselves. Knowing your role will eliminate confusion in the marriage, let the man be the man, and let the woman be the woman.

No woman wants a dictator.

Your wife is not your slave, woman was created by God to help. If we as men could do it all by ourselves, God would not have created women to be our helpmeet.

> *"18 And the LORD God said, It is not good that the man should be alone; I will make him an help meet for him."* (Genesis 2:18)

One can fix the engine while the other passes the tools. We men are the head, but we need a neck to turn the head, and that would be our wives. Husbands should allow their wives to play their Godly role, by living out what God has created them to be. Husbands, you are her husband, not her master nor her father. You are to set an example for your wife to follow. Living a life that is pleasing to God by following the example that Christ set before us. No place for dictatorship and cruelty, be affectionate to the one you say, "I do" to.

Ladies, no man wants a mother, he already has one. What is the difference between a mother and a wife? A mother helps to raise a child on Godly principles. Bringing a mother back in a husband's life is like repeating classes when you've already graduated from school. A wife is one flesh with her husband, a lifetime partner, the one who completes him. Men were created to lead, and women need a shoulder to lean on. Every team needs a coach, and every coach has a team to help win games. These are different roles that they all played, for the same purpose to achieve the same goal. God has gifted and strengthened us to run in our lane without being disqualified. Living with your spouse gives you home court advantages to help you win the game.

Wives, be your husband's greatest cheerleader, encourage him as life unfolds before your eyes. Every wife should encourage her husband to win in life, so we can all celebrate together. A wife should be a great motivator who fuels her husband's tank with love and encouragement that create sparks that light the fire in their marriage again. Husbands, while being in the role of a player remember you still need instruction from the head coach who is the God the Father of us all. Playing our roles in marriage will eliminate confusion and give us a clear path to serve without stepping on each other's toes. Running in your own lane without competing, while still being willing to finish your God-given assignment should be your goal.

Understanding your roles in marriage makes it much easier to be a team player or a lifetime partner. Seeking Godly counsel will assist you and help you to furnish the areas that are lacking or void in your marriage. Your counselor should be someone who knows God through Jesus Christ, having a personal relationship with Him with a great understanding of the scriptures.

Your role does not mean you have full control. Your role is to play the part where your spouse falls short. Playing your rightful role is setting examples for your children to follow. Remember, they are watching on the sidelines. They are taking notes in their hearts that they will one day live out in their own lives. Your role is something that is built and designed by God. Our duties are to understand these roles, seek to perfect them and be mindful of them.

We should also recognize that when playing our rightful position, we must allow our partner to learn through the process without finger pointing when they make mistakes. We all must learn how to be a better husband, wife, father, and mother as we continue in this life journey. We must discipline ourselves not to waste time finding fault with one another, but encourage each other for the good; building up each other without tearing down. Whenever we are addressing a situation or giving correction, it should be done in love, knowing that none of us is perfect and we all need God's grace and mercy. Trying to run in each other's lane will cause a collision. Trying to be who God did not create you to be will do more damage than good.

These are some tips to help you stay in your lane:

Value each other's opinion.
Keep in mind, you do not know everything.
You cannot be right all the time.
You have a partner to work with you.
Ask questions when you don't know what to do.

"21 And the eye cannot say unto the hand, I have no need of thee: nor again the head to the feet, I have no need of you." (1 Corinthians 12:21)

CHAPTER NINE

MARRIAGE IS MORE THAN SKIN DEEP

In order to go the distance in your marriage, you will have to search deeper than the skin. Outward beauty is only skin deep. To go deeper, you have to be colorblind and beware of society's cultural traps. You need to look beyond your natural vision. There are some questions you need to ask yourself: Is this the person I want to spend the rest of my life with? Check your heart to see if this is what you truly want. Can you see this person being the mother or father of your children? If you can see that you are going beyond skin deep, which is a great thing! There must be a deeper search than just the outward look.

Ask God the Father if He is pleased with your relationship and seek advice from Godly counselors. A marriage that is short-lived never goes the distance. It cannot survive with feelings alone because your feelings cannot be trusted. Skin deep relationships die easily and they cannot bear up under pressure. A relationship like this only exists because of branding. It is a show piece. No different from a movie, it is not real but used for business, looking good without being good and fashioning itself for the red carpet. What happens when the lights go off? What happens when the cameras are gone? All the glamour is good for the profile, but not for the marriage.

> *"3 Let nothing be done through strife or vainglory; but in lowliness of mind let each esteem other better than themselves."* (Philippians 2:3)

The beauty of marriage is inside out. Do not fashion the exterior and pay no attention to the interior. A skin-deep marriage is very shallow. You will surely hit rock bottom the moment you dive in because it was not designed to carry much weight. It's very hard to keep things afloat when there are so many distractions around the surface. We need to see deeper than the other eyes around us.

How do you know when your marriage is skin deep?

When those around you know more about your marriage than you do.

Are you sharing too much information with those who can't keep a secret? Check to see if this is true about your life. How can others know more than the one you said, "I do" to? A great marriage will take you to the deepest part of your spouse. Along the way you will discover things that will amaze you, things you should pray about. Remember, prayer is about agreement; but how can we pray effectively when we have a poor understanding of the relationship?

> *"7 Likewise, ye husbands, dwell with them according to knowledge, giving honour unto the wife, as unto the weaker vessel, and as being heirs together of the grace of life; that your prayers be not hindered."* (1 Peter 3:7)

We men should study our wives to gain understanding to satisfy their needs. Help them through difficult times and give them the support that will strengthen them to go the distance with us. When a relationship is skin deep, it never leaves a legacy for your bloodline. Marriage is not just about two people who are involved with each other, it's also about building families, having children, leaving a legacy for them, and fulfilling the God-given purpose for our lives.

"28 And God blessed them, and God said unto them, Be fruitful, and multiply, and replenish the earth, and subdue it: and have dominion over the fish of the sea, and over the fowl of the air, and over every living thing that moveth upon the earth." (Genesis 1:28)

God wants our marriage to flourish, prosper and mature in greatness if we apply scriptural teaching. Skin deep marriage is for the eyes, it pays no attention to the heart. It only seeks to satisfy its audience. It's like someone who prospers publicly yet fails privately. Do not settle for skin to skin, but heart to heart relationships. Go deeper with your spouse. Challenge yourself, seek to please each other and do not allow the aging of the skin to distract you from the heart. When you go beyond skin deep, you are in for the long haul. You jump from the springboard with your head pointing down to the water. This is not a belly flop or a hand catch, this is diving in with no one to stop you. To go deeper into the relationship is not settling for a skin-deep marriage.

Living beyond skin deep makes plans for the future. This is an insight far beyond what the natural eye can see, leaving the past behind and getting rid of dead history that prevents us from moving forward. We need to discipline ourselves to live on Godly principles. Preparing for the next level with anticipation and the new pages of life's journey will bring us closer to our goal. Living beyond skin deep displays a deeper intimacy in your marriage.

A woman of noble character is admirable, and her strength is revealed through her hospitality. This kind of character protects her reputation and covers her shortcomings. When you seek to clothe the interior with love that display Godly character, your life will always be on the lips of others.

> *"28 Her children arise up, and call her blessed; her husband also, and he praiseth her.29 Many daughters have done virtuously, but thou excellest them all"* (Proverbs 31:28-29)

This is a perfect example of a wife living beyond skin deep. You will leave a legacy that outlives you and transcends through generations to come. Your skin is not your true identity, it must not define you, we need to go deeper. A skin deep marriage is all about the show, satisfying the appetite of the viewers but turns a blind eye to the marriage. Skin deep marriage is nothing but a fashion show that lives for the runway, placing no value on the home but for the cameras. Not willing to consistently sacrifice for the family but living for the moment and disregarding the future. Many marriages are damaged because of skin deep relationships, they seek applause not purpose. When the show is over, silence and loneliness are the only companion you have standing with you. No hands to hold, no shoulder to lean on, the marriage is stifling and gasping for air while waiting for the next episode.

There is still hope even for skin deep marriages, you can turn things around if you are willing to invite God as a partner in your relationship. Repentance and prayer are the first steps to a resolution. This sets the stage for God to do His work in your marriage. When you approach things with a spirit of humility you will not be overlooked. Humility removes the pointing of fingers; it removes the blame game and show us how far we are from perfection. Acknowledging your weaknesses before God invites His power to work in you. We must always bear in mind that He is limitless, and we are limited. He is the Creator, and we are the created. He knows all things; we are nothing without Him. There is nothing that is too hard for Him to fix, He is the God of the impossible.

Seek to have a heart-to-heart conversation with your spouse. Quite often people think that it is not important, so they run away rather than facing the issue head on. Confrontation is a very interesting word that many ears are afraid to hear. Confrontation demands answers to unresolved situations. Confrontation can also lead to further problems if your approach is not motivated by love.

We must put pride aside and confront each other, not pointing fingers but taking responsibility for our own behaviors. We must be accountable to each other, which will lead to a marriage beyond the surface of the skin. Seeds that become trees develop roots when they are planted beneath the surface. The seed grabs hold of the soil which absorbs water to sustain the tree so that it bears fruit. Relationships that go beyond skin deep involve planting and rooting in each other. Look for the best in each other, then go after what you see and invest yourself there.

The skin of a person cannot tell you anything about the soul or the heart of that person. A house is not a home without someone living in it. You have to make it a home by sharing the love of God and carefully furnishing every part for the comfort of each other. Skin deep relationships are short-lived and are self-centered. It is the world's way of loving, not God's way. True relationships take time, effort, and great sacrifice. You will never be disappointed if you challenge yourself to go deeper in your relationship.

When a marriage is only skin deep it can breed speculations that lead to false accusations. This is when your eyes are only focusing on the exterior and not being sensitive to the interior. You can overlook moments that you should pay close attention to. That's a very shallow and hollow way of life, living on the surface without understanding.

Speculation plants seeds for division, awakens contention, and invites divorce.

For example, if your spouse asks, "Where are you going?" Your answer should be honest and forthright. In case of an emergency, the information of your location should be known for your own safety. You should always have access to each other's whereabouts which initiates trust and avoids speculations. One flesh carries no secrets and no hidden agendas. If you are on the phone having what appears to be a private conversation with someone and your spouse sits beside you, the conversation should not stop without an explanation. The right thing to do before you act is to explain why you need privacy for that conversation. It could be that you are trying to avoid noise while talking or you don't want to be distracted because of the nature of the conversation. Being honest and forthright will kill the seed of speculation and bring forth understanding. When you allow pride to get the better of you, it's a sure fall that provides no cushion. If you dig beneath the surface of millions of failed marriages, you will see the real root, which is failing to communicate. Seeds of speculation can easily be uprooted if you are willing to conquer your mountain of pride and confront the real issues.

Always practice transparency with your spouse and free yourself from a life of secrecy. Live in harmony with one another so when mistakes do happen it will not be too late for correcting and resolving a situation. Understanding will lead to freedom and ignorance can lead to imprisonment. Your marriage should go deeper than the skin because it has nothing to do with your complexion. The source of your marriage is not your culture or your background, it is through God Himself. Skin deep marriage can be a great cover-up, but can make your marriage vulnerable to attacks.

CHAPTER TEN

TOXIC PRESSURE

In order to live, we must inhale and exhale. The same holds true for marriages. Expressive communication keeps the life of the marriage healthy. Even venting sometimes is helpful when done in a mature way. When a husband or wife exercises self-expression yet deprives their spouse of the same privilege, this threatens the life of the marriage. It is like breathing out and never breathing in… It suffocates your marriage, leaving it with little chance of survival.

Four problems arise when self-expression is not exercised in the marriage:

1. You will come to a boiling point (layers of unresolved issues begin floating on the surface of your marriage)
2. Every part of you will be leaking (everyone can witness your indiscretions)
3. A great explosion (outburst of anger that could damage the relationship with your spouse and others as well)
4. Not being able to talk about what you dislike can become a resentment.

Marriage toxicity is like a garbage truck traveling from house to house picking up garbage, pressing it deep in the container with an iron arm, compressing to make room for more trash to fit in. If the truck is not unloaded, those who around you will know because of the stench that no one can bear. So is the stench of a toxic marriage. A marriage built on denial without confrontation will die. Those who keep everything inside without expressing them will reach a boiling point. You will see the sadness on their faces, change in their attitudes which causes discomfort to others around them.

Healthy communication will help any marriage from decaying. Allow your spouse to express themselves by releasing what's stored up inside of them. Don't allow bitterness to take root and bear the wrong kind of fruit. No one likes pressure, why keep it? Everyone has the desire to express themselves, they deserve that freedom. When I understand you and you understand me, we will know how to make the necessary adjustments to build a healthy marriage. Too much pressure can lead to chronic depression, mental illness, suicide, and the list goes on.

How do we safeguard ourselves from the poison that damages relationships?

Do not allow your mind to be a storehouse of mental garbage.

Do not procrastinate, unload your problems in prayer. Remember, God is the healer, the one who loves and deeply cares for us his children.

"7 Casting all your care upon him; for he careth for you." (1 Peter 5:7)

Why not replace pressure with purpose and pain with progress?

Marriage is freedom not slavery. It should be fun, not a war zone. The reason why so many marriages fail is because they are too hard on themselves. At times we mistreat and deprive ourselves of things we truly deserve, taking what is sacred for granted, shifting our attention to things that seem more important. Whatever you don't feed will starve, whatever you leave in the open becomes a target which gives the enemy a clear shot by letting down your guard. Some argue and complain about feeling isolated, when they created the distance between themselves by not spending time with each other. When we are hungry, we find something to eat; when we are thirsty, we find something to drink. The same principles apply to married life. Taking a break is necessary even when you are consumed with life's pressures. Spending time with God in prayer will help you overcome whatever your challenges are. Making time for each other can greatly enhance the quality of your marriage.

A wounded soldier is not fit for war. Unresolved pressure can also wound your marriage. We cannot allow ourselves to be overwhelmed with pressure. Living with ongoing fear, anxiety, and worrying can kick the life out of marriage. Present all worries to God along with the stress that comes with it. Live a life with balance, and you will see great results. We serve a Father who loves us and deeply cares about our affairs in life. Seek Him always.

If you have children, be there for them. Do not ignore your parental responsibilities. We are limited, but God is limitless, and nothing is impossible with Him. A life of constant pressure is a distraction, that could cause you to lose focus and to ignore present responsibilities. Give honor and respect to each other by acknowledging each other's needs. This encourages a balanced married life.

When was the last time you said, "I love you"? Is this sentiment past due? How could something that was so right become so wrong?

Perhaps one of the following could be the answer:

- The sentimental expiration date has been ignored.
- You turned your attention away from what was important.
- You refused to yield from allowing your spouse to express themselves.

When was the last time you made affectionate love? When was the last time you said, "Thank you"? When was the last time you had a heart-to-heart talk? When was the last time you surprised your spouse with something nice? Take full control of your marriage relationship by going back to the foundation of love and rebuild from there. Say thank you to one another. Express your love for each other. Repaying past due commitments to each other can bring back the sparks in your marriage. Make every effort to live a balanced life that is not consumed with unnecessary pressure and strengthen the marriage for the long haul by the grace of God.

What can cause unnecessary pressure?

- Taking on someone else's problems that have nothing to do with you.
- Not allowing others to help you when you need it.
- Being the spokesperson for everyone, trying to lead where you should follow.
- Thinking that nothing gets done without you.

Your input is necessary in some situations, but if we are not careful, we can also create a mess that does not belong to us and invite toxic pressure. These overcompensations strain the marriage, what rightfully belongs to each other. Unwanted pressure can create weapons in your marriage that cut without mercy, causing division with no sense of direction. This encourages unhealthy conversations, destroying communication, and causing a lifetime of wounds. Intense pressure can lead to a bed of frustration. A frustrated tongue can become a destructive instrument cutting deep into the layers of the fabric of our marriage. A divided marriage is a death sentence. It will kill relationships, families, and destinies.

I recommend:

- Spend each day with God in prayer and devotion.
- Take each day as it comes.
- Live each day like it's your last.
- Spend each day with God and your spouse.
- Do not take any day for granted; every day is important.
- A life of toxic pressure can lead to an eggshell life style.

What is an eggshell lifestyle?

It is like a ticking time-bomb, one soft step can create an outburst or an explosion. A life without substance cracks like an eggshell under slight pressure. This type of marriage is unsuccessful because the consequences are so overwhelming and difficult to deal with. When feelings and emotions are dominant, it is like walking on eggshells in your relationship. A refusal to communicate pushes each other away to avoid punishing arguments, but this only creates more pressure. An eggshell marriage cannot withstand pressure, this can lead to a spiteful reaction that could last for months and in some cases years. If we do not seek direction to remove the toxic junk from our lives the eggshell lifestyle is a sure shot.

This scripture teaches us how to conduct ourselves among each other, because of what Christ did for us.

*"**13** Forbearing one another, and forgiving one another, if any man have a quarrel against any: even as Christ forgave you, so also do ye."* (Colossians 3:13)

The scriptures are clear on how we should live as God's children. Marriage should be inspired with love not hatred.

One of the worst dangers for a soldier is to find themselves in a minefield, where each step threatens their life; any move could be their last. Knowing where the hidden bombs are planted could give a better chance of survival to get out alive. Such is the case with an eggshell marriage. The slightest offense can tick you off like a bomb, causing you to explode against the one you declared the love of your life. An eggshell marriage breeds spiteful reactions. This can cause excruciating pain and damage to the relationship leaving each party wounded and feeling helpless. This can make you a permanent victim to your own circumstances.

Some wives are deprived of money, gifts, and attention from their husbands, because of unresolved hurts of the past. The same is true for husbands who lose sexual privileges from their wives, often opening doors to outside temptation. We shouldn't hold onto or penalize our spouse for past hurts. Marriage is not for perfect people; it's designed for couples to grow and mature. Marriage is the perfect arrangement to express God's given agape love towards each other, manifesting the Father's love through Jesus Christ. Unfulfilled marriages void of attention and absent of great memories are the result of toxic pressure. At times finger-pointing and fault-finding take the place of love. Neither party wants to be wrong but claims to be right. The relationship becomes competitive, argumentative, and extremely abusive to the point they can't stand to be around each other. Patience goes through the roof and resentment moves into the home. There is no longer tolerance for each other because of being burnt out and frustrated. You can silently grow apart and drift away unknowingly, until the reality of this lifestyle catches up with you. This is when an eggshell lifestyle introduces itself into your marriage. The least words can crack you open and result in an outburst, causing rage and anger because you have no more strength to withstand any more pressure.

How can this be avoided?

It takes two people in agreement to get things done; it cannot be one-sided. Oftentimes when a marriage fails, it's because one party allows pride to build a wall between them. The first option is to repent before God and apologize to each other.

> *"16 Confess your faults one to another, and pray one for another, that ye may be healed. The effectual fervent prayer of a righteous man availeth much."* (James 5:16)

Be sensitive to each other's feelings, and knowledgeable of each other's situation. Take the initiative and time to find out why your spouse is acting out. Give your spouse the space to express themselves by releasing what may be trapped inside. Recognize that this is not all about you. Your marriage consists of two before God.

An eggshell marriage is one of the most difficult marriages to live in. It's lonely, empty, very sad and extremely boring. At any time, anything can trigger an argument. One wrong word can crack a person's shell or crush a person if there is nothing to withstand the pressure. Most people don't take an eggshell life-style seriously until it's too late and becomes cancerous. When the cancerous marriage spills over into the lives of friends, relatives, or even children, it's obvious the marriage has lost its chemistry.

Upbringing could be the root cause of an eggshell lifestyle. This is more common in relationships than you think. Each person should do an examination of themselves and their family history. Remember, God doesn't reveal your full life to you at once. This is why seeking Godly counsel is wise. It's up to you to accept this truth. Wife, there is a part of you that your husband sees that you don't know. Husband, there is a part of you that your wife sees that you don't recognize. God can reveal these areas of your lives if you seek Him in each other.

"15 The way of a fool is right in his own eyes, But he who heeds counsel is wise." (Proverbs 12:15)

No one is right all the time or sees and knows everything. Only God has that power and ability. Do not allow your feelings to become your god. Live a life that follows the Word of God, not your opinions or ideas. Do not allow your emotions to run over you. Emotions can play a great role in your life, but the key is to know what that role is. Emotions were given to us by God to express our feelings about Him. We praise and worship God with tears of joy and admiration. We express our hearts to Him because He loves us far beyond our imagination. Emotions are great when monitored appropriately.

We use this same God-given emotion to express how we feel about our spouse. This is why we hug, we kiss, we make love, we cry together and embrace each other. Emotional affection is a driving force in marriage. Our emotions can also express how we feel about ungodly behavior, but in those moments we have to apply self-control.

"26 Be ye angry, and sin not: let not the sun go down upon your wrath." (Ephesians 4:26)

We have the right to be angry, but we do not have the right to sin. Let God's words navigate your marriage, then you will find joy and peace overflowing in your life.

Continue cultivating substance in your marriage. Pray together and seek God's word for instructions. Stop trying to win an argument but rather seek to resolve it. Take time out to have clean fun. Compliment each other, celebrate together in every step of progress you see in your marriage. Speak to each other gracefully and respectfully. Live for purpose, not for people. Plan for the future and stop looking back at the past. Treat each other fairly, not with bias or partial regard.

"6 Let your speech be always with grace, seasoned with salt, that ye may know how ye ought to answer every man." (Colossians 4:6)

What are some things you should be aware of?

Do not allow your siblings to wedge you out. Your extended family must always have a place in your life, but marriage is priority.

"24 Therefore shall a man leave his father and his mother, and shall cleave unto his wife: and they shall be one flesh." (Genesis 2:24)

"9 What therefore God hath joined together, let not man put asunder." (Mark 10:9)

Exercise boundaries, protocols, and self-discipline: To do the right thing, create a healthy and loving marriage to the Glory of God. Keep your marriage respectful, don't take each other for granted. Marriage is a lifetime investment, and you are the investors. Monitor your investment, and do not lose sight of its equity.

Foundation of love building blocks:

Respect:
Displays value
Shows importance
Handle with care
Set boundaries

Honesty:
Keep things glued together
Paves the way for loyalty
Births assurance

Trust:
Creates chemistry
Invites peace
Dismantles insecurity

These buildings blocks will prevent you from saying I DON'T and encourage I DO.

Ask yourself who did you marry?

I am very sure you did not say I DO to your money.
I am absolutely sure you did say I DO to your dreams.
I am convinced that you did not say I DO to your families or friends or your career.

You said I DO to the person who stood before you on that wedding day.

The very vows you said, "until death do us part," always keep them in consideration before you make an emotional decision. If you find yourself struggling through an eggshell moment in your marriage, it's not too late to make necessary adjustments.

Spend Quality Time

This helps you to examine yourself and welcome change. Do not be quick to point fingers to divert attention from yourself. Spend devotional time with God through prayer and studying of His word, this will help to mature and grow in His love.

Capitalize on the Moment

Life is made of years and moments…time waits on no one. God's given moments is an opportunity within time. Your time may not be the right time, but God's timing, is always the perfect time.

Don't Overlook the Possibilities

Keep your eyes open to each of them, but only take the good with you. You don't have to cheat on each other to end a marriage, just ignoring each other long enough will do the job for you. Choose the way that God designed for you and free yourself from toxic junk that leads to an eggshell marriage.

Look for Warning Signs

Witnessing failed marriages, thinking it cannot happen to you is deceiving yourself…this should be a warning to you. If spending time with each other is another holiday and fighting and quarreling becomes the norm, these are warning signs that leads to a life of cycles revolving around the same situation over and over again. Believing others instead of your spouse and never taking time to listen to each other are also warning signs.

Don't Allow Past Mistakes to Navigate your Future

Not learning from your past mistakes will repeat itself in your future. This perpetuates a life of negative cycles. There is great hope if you put your faith and trust in the Lord Jesus to carry you through those situations. Give your heart and soul to Him and let the Holy Spirit guide you constantly. Let His word fill your heart and let it wash your mind daily. He wants the best for you always.

My wife and I have been together for over 37 years, we learned the hard way, we made mistakes like everyone else; but we also learned how to allow God to fight those battles for us. I can say today that He did, and He will continue to fight those battles for us. Be encouraged and take good care of each other in Jesus' name.

Praying, studying the Word of God together, communicating with each other, and working on issues as they appear will without a doubt keep your marriage free of any thoughts of separation or divorce.

CONCLUSION

How do we address these situations?

By inviting solutions through understanding. We must come together in one common belief that we both see things differently sometimes. Every marriage has its own problems, but we must not allow these things to fester.

Sometimes the problem is in your finances or an affair with someone. Struggles can start through family members, or your own children. These things must be tackled and addressed before it become cancerous. Once it becomes cancerous, it's more than a problem but a condition.

There is a difference between a problem and a state. If you should be asked by someone, "How is your marriage?" and you say, "We have problems!" That is not telling the person the state of your marriage. A problem can be one or two things, but a state speaks of the condition of the marriage. When you have a problem, oftentimes you can mask it and work it out without your family or friends' knowing. It is good to keep things private and try to resolve things through your pastor or one who you trust that walks in Godly wisdom.

When the marriage is in a bad state, it's no longer just a problem but a condition. It is dead, or on life support and deteriorating to the point that no mask can fix it. It must be uncovered not to the world but to a trusted leader, counselor, or someone else that

God leads you to, who will help bring back the fruitfulness and life in your marriage. We should not treat a problem like a condition. They are not the same. When you can cover some problems and work them out privately, you cannot mask or cover a marriage that is in a bad state. You need wise counseling from Godly counselors that's filled with wisdom to help you. Keeping everything a secret can expose you to the public. Being open and transparent will keep you from disgrace.

"14 Where no counsel is, the people fall: but in the multitude of counsellors there is safety." (Proverbs 11:14)

Seek God first in all things, let Him guide you. Be steadfast in prayer, serve and love one another. Invest in each other; in this way, you will disassemble lack and stagnancy, making room for peace, love, and affection to reign. May the Lord Bless you all, in Jesus' name.

PICTORIAL

"Husbands, love your wives, even as Christ also loved the church, and gave himself for it; That he might sanctify and cleanse it with the washing of water by the word, That he might present it to himself a glorious church, not having spot, or wrinkle, or any such thing; but that it should be holy and without blemish. So ought men to love their wives as their own bodies. He that loveth his wife loveth himself. For no man ever yet hated his own flesh, but nourisheth and cherisheth it, even as the Lord the church:"

(Ephesians 5:25-29)

"Two are better than one; because they have a good reward for their labour. For if they fall, the one will lift up his fellow: but woe to him that is alone when he falleth; for he hath not another to help him up. Again, if two lie together, then they have heat: but how can one be warm alone?"

(Ecclesiastes 4:9-11)

"So God created man in his own image, in the image of God created he him; male and female created he them. And God blessed them, and God said to them, Be fruitful, and multiply, and replenish the earth, and subdue it: and have dominion over the fish of the sea, and over the fowl of the air, and over every living thing that moveth upon the earth."

(Genesis 1:27-28)

"Husbands, love your wives, even as Christ also loved the church, and gave himself for it," (Ephesians 5:25)

For Speaking Engagements, Book Signings,
Appearances, and Interviews,

Contact:

Beloved Group
Email: belovedgrp@gmail.com
Phone: (786) 408-2992

Address:
P.O. Box 451897
Sunrise, Florida 33345

Website:
http://belovedgrp.com/
FaceBook: m.facebook.com/BelovedGroup
Instagram: instagram.com/groupbeloved/
Twitter: twitter.com/GroupLoved

Made in the USA
Columbia, SC
16 October 2022

69474860R00050